T595

11-20-02

Happy Birthday
to Hannah, our
dearest Connecticut Yankee!
Love,
Papa + Dagsa

CONNECTICUT

A Picture Book to Remember Her by

CRESCENT BOOKS
NEW YORK

CLB 877
© Illustrations and text: Colour Library Books Ltd.,
  Guildford, Surrey, England.
Text filmsetting by Acesetters Ltd., Richmond, Surrey, England.
Printed in Spain.
1985 edition published by Crescent Books, distributed by Crown Publishers, Inc.
ISBN 0 517 477874
h g f e d c b a

Anyone trying to convey a sense of small-town America can do it by calling the small town "Podunk." Though there is no such town, the name was given to a tribe of Indians living in the beautiful Connecticut River Valley in 1614 by the Dutch explorer Adriaen Block, the first European to visit there. By the time English settlers arrived from the Massachusetts colony 20 years later, the Dutch already had a tenuous claim on the place and an outpost of New Amsterdam on the site of what is now Hartford.

The tension between the two groups gave the American English language another pair of words. The Dutch were outnumbered and frightened to the point of building a wall at the north end of their colony, on Manhattan Island, to keep the English out. The site is known everywhere in the world today as Wall Street. But wall or no, the Dutch knew in their hearts that it was only a matter of time before their Connecticut neighbors would overrun them and they covered their fears with a bravado that, to them at least, passed for wit. The English were known as "John Bull" even then, and Peter Stuyvesant's followers thought it was great fun to mock them as "John Cheese" whenever they had an encounter. In their language, John Cheese is "Jon Quese," which to British ears came out as "Yankee," a word Connecticut people used all over New England to describe themselves.

Nearness to New York has always loomed large in the development of Connecticut. Though never really great farming country, the hills and valleys, the northern coast of Long Island Sound, are strikingly beautiful and almost from the beginning wealthy New Yorkers were lured there in search of a house in the country.

The result, in part at least, is that though Connecticut is one of the smallest of the states, its per-capita income is one of the highest. It has become corporate headquarters to some of America's biggest companies, too, and its rolling hills are as much dotted with stainless steel and glass as with the quaint stone walls that have been a Connecticut institution since the earliest days.

After Yale University settled down in New Haven in 1716, the state became a haven for education and Connecticut is home to many of the best prep schools in the country, where future Ivy Leaguers get a head start not only on their education, but on their social contacts as well.

Before the Revolution, England's government placed restrictions on the amount of manufacturing that could be done in Connecticut. The Connecticut Yankees got even during the war, when they became the new country's biggest producer of arms and ammunition. Samuel Colt, inventor of the "gun that won the West," started his career in Hartford; the Winchester company in New Haven provided the long rifles. And that may be one reason why Hartford has been America's insurance capital for generations.

Facing page: woodland and pond at Sharon.

Top left: the Old State House, Hartford, designed by Charles Bulfinch. The first session of the General Assembly to be held in Connecticut's present State Capitol (above) was convened in 1879. Top right: Hartford's Hilton Hotel, and (right) the crenellated walls of Wadsworth Atheneum. Facing page: the State Capitol overlooks Bushnell Memorial Park, Hartford.

More than 40,000 art objects, from ancient Egyptian artifacts, through 19th century French paintings to contemporary sculpture (top and above right) are exhibited in the five connected buildings of the Wadsworth Atheneum (this page). Facing page: Alexander Calder's "Stegosaurus", a metal stabile outside the Wadsworth Atheneum.

Noah Webster House (left, below and bottom), birthplace of the statesman, lawyer and compiler of the *American Dictionary*, is a fine, 18th-century farmhouse in West Hartford which has been restored and authentically furnished in pre-revolutionary style. Facing page: clapboard houses near Elizabeth Park in Hartford.

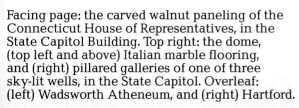

Facing page: the carved walnut paneling of the Connecticut House of Representatives, in the State Capitol Building. Top right: the dome, (top left and above) Italian marble flooring, and (right) pillared galleries of one of three sky-lit wells, in the State Capitol. Overleaf: (left) Wadsworth Atheneum, and (right) Hartford.

Top and overleaf, right: the drawing room, (left) the conservatory, (above) the nursery, and (overleaf, left) the dining room of Mark Twain's house (facing page), Hartford.

Top: farm buildings near West Granby, and (right) Old Newgate Prison, East Granby. Above: house and garden in Windsor. Facing page: early aircraft exhibited in the New England Air Museum at Windsor Locks.

MARQUIT RICKENBERG SPECIAL
1934

PRATT & WHITNEY
TWIN WASP JR.

HAMILTON STANDARD
CONSTANT SPEED PROPELLER

COLONIAL
AIR LINES

DYNDIUK SPORT
1934

ALEXANDER DYNDIUK, A SKILLED SOUTHINGTON, CONN. MACHINIST,
DESIGNED HIS "SPORT" ALONG THE POPULAR "DEATH PARASOL" LINES.
ASSISTED BY HIS WIFE, JENNIE, HE BEGAN CONSTRUCTION IN 1930
USING METAL STRUCTURE THROUGHOUT AND A UNIQUELY CONVERTED
AIR-COOLED FORD MODEL "A" ENGINE.   COMPLETED IN JANUARY, 1934,
HE SUCCESSFULLY FLEW THE AIRCRAFT TWICE.   REPORTEDLY
ACCOMPLISHING LOOPS AND OTHER MANEUVERS.   HE NEVER FLEW
AGAIN.   HE DISMANTLED AND STORED

MAINTAINED BY SHARON DEVEAU

Left: the original Hitchcock Chair Factory, Riverton, built by Lambert Hitchcock in 1826. Top right and facing page: chairs in the Hitchcock Museum (top left), housed in an 1829 church. Above: clapboard house, Riverton. Overleaf: fishing, (left) near North Colebrook, and (right) in the Farmington River.

Elegant white clapboard in the town of
Norfolk (facing page and top), in the centre
of Colebrook (above), and on the green in
Winchester (right).

Bottom right: the main hall, and (remaining pictures) the parlour, of the Hotchkiss-Fyler House in Torrington, built at the turn of the century by Orsamus Roman Fyler. Facing page: Litchfield, where (top) the Congregational Church is set on Litchfield green. (Bottom left) the Town Hall.

Top: a Mexican and Civil War memorial, Cornwall Hollow, (above left) West Cornwall, and (facing page) a covered bridge at West Cornwall. Above right: the Ragamont Inn, Salisbury.

These pages: green, well-watered Connecticut countryside. Facing page: pond and mixed woodland outside Sharon, (bottom left) geese near Cornwall Bridge, and (bottom right) footbridge over a pond, Salisbury.

Top left: the public library, and (above) a house and store, New Milford. Facing page, bottom right: the masts of the *HMS Rose*, a replica of the British war frigate whose success prompted colonists to found the American navy during the Revolutionary War, rise above Captain Cove's Marina (this page, top right), Bridgeport. Facing page, remaining pictures: the harborfront at Captain's Cove, Bridgeport.

Top right: Morse College, a 1960s addition to
Yale University, New Haven, which was founded
in 1701. Top left: mobile outside the
Beinecke Rare Book and Manuscript Library
(above), and (left and facing page) interiors
of the Memorial Hall, Yale University.

WORLD WAR II

VIETNAM

EXIT

TO THE MEN OF YALE
WHO GAVE THEIR LIVES IN THE SERVICE OF THEIR COUNTRY
DURING THE GREAT WORLD WARS
THE UNIVERSITY HAS DEDICATED THIS MEMORIAL
THAT THEIR HIGH DEVOTION MAY PASS TO
OTHERS AS A LIVING FIRE

O youth foregone, foregoing!
O dreams unseen, unsought!
God give you joy of knowing
What life your death has bought"

These pages: the ivy-clad walls and stone-mullioned, leaded windows of Yale University. The University was named for Elihu Yale, a benefactor who, in 1718, made a substantial donation to what was then a college. The institution attained university status in 1887.

Several thousand students study in the
apparent quiet of Yale University campus
(below and bottom right). Bottom left and
facing page: Yale Old Campus, and (right)
New Haven Green.

Facing page: the Shore Line Trolley Museum in East Haven offers rides in lovingly-restored trolley cars of the 19th century. Top: New Haven Green, (above left) New Haven, and (above right) a shaded street near Yale University. The American Clock and Watch Museum (overleaf), Bristol, is housed largely in the Miles Lewis House, built in 1801, and gives a vivid account of the history of American horology.

Top left: church service, and (above right) a store, in Rocky Hill. Top right: falls near Hampton, and (above left) a newly-cut hayfield outside Bolton. Facing page: sapling birch trees grow beside a mill pond, Middletown.

These pages: brightly-colored hot-air balloons are made ready to ascend at a balloon meet in Bristol. Top: intricate decorations based on the distinctive, late 18th-century design of a Montgolfier balloon.

The mansion that is now the Hill-Stead Museum (below), Farmington, was designed in 1901 by Theodate Pope and Stanford White as a home for Theodate's wealthy parents. Remaining pictures: largely original furnishings inside the Hill-Stead Museum. Overleaf: (left) a clapboard house with ornate tower, East Hampton, and (right) Wadsworth Falls Park.

Top left: pleasure-boats at Mystic Seaport Museum, and (top right) Bashan Falls, near Moodus. Gillette Castle (above left), outside Hadlyme, was built overlooking the Connecticut River by the unorthodox actor and playwright William Hooker Gillette in 1915. Above right: encroaching woodland in Devils Hopyard State Park. Facing page: Goodspeed Opera House (top), at East Haddam on the Connecticut River, was completed in 1876. Bottom left and bottom right: houses in the center of Chester.

Top: Essex Marina, on the Connecticut River. Left and above: pleasant, spacious houses in Essex, and (facing page) house and grounds bordered by a stream near Essex.

Top: war memorial on the green in Old
Mystic Village (above and right) a replica
of a colonial settlement. Facing page:
quiet streets in Essex. Overleaf: (left) a
stream, and (right) still water, near Old
Mystic Village.

Top: Mystic River. In the 19th century the
site now occupied by Mystic Seaport Museum
(remaining pictures) housed the thriving
shipyard of George Greenman & Co. Today,
the museum's reconstructed period
buildings and preserved and replica
sailing vessels reproduce the atmosphere
of a 19th century seaport.

Top, above and facing page: Mystic Seaport Museum. Right: Mystic town. Overleaf: the restored wooden whaleship *Charles W. Morgan,* Mystic Seaport Museum.